To: Dan
From: Dad
Christmas 2006

Study the best on your
journey to greater
Leadership skills !

THE 12 LEADERSHIP PRINCIPLES

OF

DEAN SMITH

Second, I believe he wanted a similar excellence of speech from us. While I was in his office, he expressed disappointment in a former player's recent book, which contained some profanity. He was pleased with the book, but disdained the language. Cursing represented a poverty of vocabulary, and he wanted the best for himself and his players. Do we as leaders desire this same kind of excellence in our own personal appearance and our speech from those who work with us?

I've already related to you my close call with Coach Smith regarding his insistence on punctuality. He felt that being tardy was stealing — stealing another person's time. It didn't matter who you were, superstar or sub, if you weren't on time, there would be a consequence. He knew bosses wouldn't tolerate it later on, and he felt he needed to teach it now.

Woody Durham tells this story. "I remember one of the first times we went to Princeton. I was doing his TV show. He and I flew together, and we went to the hotel in time to catch the bus to practice. But the hotel clerk accidentally gave me the wrong room key. I remember it vividly. We were at the Howard Johnson's on the New Jersey turnpike. I yelled at him that I still had to get another key, and to have the bus wait for me because I'd just be a second. But when I walked outside to get on the bus, it was gone. He wouldn't wait for the president of the United States."

Donald Williams was almost late for the pre-game meal in the 1993 championship game. When he arrived Coach Smith said, "You're eight seconds ahead of the time limit." Williams, of course, started the game and was the hero, one of the prime reasons Carolina won the national championship. However, if he had been one second late, he would not have started the national championship game. And it was his watch that determined tardiness!

Is this a silly rule? Is it the dictates of a control freak? Or is it a key principle of a man who knows how the world operates and is committed to making young men into people of character? I think it is the latter.

I also demand that staff people be on time for meetings. I once had an intern who had an especially hard time doing this. I kept pushing him. Later I found out he told someone else that he did not have a positive experience on our staff because he always had to be on time. He failed to understand the importance of punctuality. He also struggled with it as he moved on to another job.

Are we leaders committed to teaching our underlings, especially younger ones, the value of punctuality? Do we believe we are stealing someone's time when we're late?

Honesty and Integrity

Another character trait that causes Dean Smith to stand out from the crowd is his absolute refusal to cheat. His unfailing honesty and integrity truly set him apart.

Andrew Carnegie once said, "As I grow older, I pay less attention to what men say. I just watch what they do." If you watch Coach Smith for a long time, you'll see that his words match up with his deeds in all of life's situations.

The dictionary defines integrity as "the state of being complete, unified." The opposite of integrity is duplicity and hypocrisy.

When I was a senior in high school, Coach Smith came down to Orlando, Florida, to recruit me. We went to eat at a well-known eating establishment at the Orlando airport; it happened to be owned and operated by one of my father's close friends.

When we finished our meal, Coach Smith asked for the check. My dad's friend came to the table and said dinner was on the house. Coach Smith objected. Dad's friend insisted. Coach Smith objected even more vociferously. The resistance continued.

Finally, Coach Smith said that this could be breaking NCAA rules and he could not permit it. My dad's friend finally yielded. This story shows how Smith was able to coach for 35 years and not once have the smell of scandal taint his program. Honesty was an absolutely essential life principle for him.

Coach Guthridge gave me another illustration that demonstrates the same truth. If Coach Smith ever played golf with someone who cheated — moved their ball unfairly in the rough, inched the ball a bit closer on the green — he would simply walk off the golf course and never play with that person again. He demanded honesty from himself and those around him. He was not a cheater and he refused to play with one. Roy Williams told me that unless the golf ball is hanging on the edge of the hole, Dean Smith will make you putt it out. "He would always say, 'How do I know you can make that putt? Make it and prove to me you're a good golfer.'"

Coach Smith steadfastly refused to cheat. He made that decision before he ever accepted the job as head coach at North Carolina. When he was hired, the chancellor told him to run a clean program and recruit able scholar-athletes. Winning was not the highest priority. Therefore, the decision to cheat was never a temptation. But I don't think it had to be. His own personal character would not allow him to cheat under any circumstances.

I must admit some incredulity about this. How could a contemporary coach win and *not* cheat? So I asked John Swofford, the athletic director over Coach Smith for 17 years, if it were true that Smith never cheated. He replied, "Nothing you could put in the category of cheating at all. You know, if you've ever looked at the NCAA rule book, and the thickness of it, there are all kinds of things on which you could stub your toe. But anytime there was a question at North Carolina in terms of a violation, we would turn it into the NCAA immediately. We were never investigated. Nothing of any substance was ever unearthed. That's because of Dean's absolute commitment to run a clean program."

Eddie Fogler, present coach at the University of South Carolina, offered this perspective. "Even though he had intense rivalries, I don't think any opposing coach would ever believe that Dean Smith would violate an NCAA rule. He is that well thought of among his peers. They know his integrity and honesty. That is the way he has always done it.

"One thing that especially bothered him was the suggestion that he didn't have to recruit players, that he could simply select the ones he wanted. He often interpreted that to mean that if his teams weren't good, or if he didn't coach at a great school, that perhaps he would cheat. Well, Coach Smith could be at the worst school at the bottom of the best conference and there is no way he would ever violate NCAA rules. If he lost his job because of his refusal to cheat, then he would lose his job."

I asked Swofford if this commitment to honesty positively influenced other parts of the athletic program. "Of course!" he responded quickly. "The way he ran the basketball program had a tremendous influence on the rest of the athletic program. He set the standard of integrity. Because of his commitment to academics over athletics, his incredible graduation rate, the way his players loved him, the way he treated people, and his refusal to cheat, he set the bar for the other departments. In fact, whenever we interviewed a coach in another sport, we would point to the basketball program as an example of what can be done and how we want it to be done. I used his extraordinary honesty and success to challenge other divisions. Not only did it work, but it produced an excellence among us all. It's one of, if not the major reason we regularly won the nation's all-sports trophy."

Woody Durham even suggested that Coach Smith's overwhelming commitment to honesty may have been one of the reasons he ultimately retired. When I asked him to explain, he said, "There is such a huge commitment by Coach Smith to play by the rules. He would never counsel his big men, even if they were 6'9" and weighed 270 pounds, to use their strength wrongly if it were against the rules."

One of the most publicized encounters Coach Smith ever had with a rival coach was with Rick Barnes (who was then at Clemson, now Texas) in the opening round of the ACC Tournament a few years ago. A Clemson player had undercut UNC superstar Jerry Stackhouse. Coach Smith went after the player and Coach Barnes. From Coach Smith's standpoint, I think it had little to do with protecting his players, as the press suggested. It had nothing to do, in my opinion, with a personal vendetta against Rick Barnes. It had everything to do with the way Coach Smith thought the game should be played. When the Clemson player undercut Stackhouse, yes, Coach Smith was concerned with Stackhouse's well-being. But he was much more concerned with the game not being played the way the rules stated.

"He sincerely regretted the confrontation after it happened," Durham told me. "But he was saying to the official and everyone, 'Hey, there are rules, a book, and a way the game is supposed to be played. This is not the way the game was designed to be played.'"

Reflecting on Coach Smith's love for the way the game should be played and how it had changed over the years, Durham concluded, "I think he became frustrated that the rules were not being followed, and it helped motivate him to retire."

Leaders, is honesty important to you? Is being above reproach essential to your leadership? Will you refuse to deal with anyone who bends or breaks the rules to succeed? Parents teach their children that honesty is the best policy. Coach Smith believed and practiced this maxim at all times.

Learning How to Be Under Authority

Before I began my ministry, I had the privilege of visiting with a prominent person in religious circles. Desiring success, I asked him what I needed to do first to pave my path to personal achievement. His answer surprised me. He said, "Go serve in someone else's ministry. Learn how to help him succeed. Learn how to be under authority. Then you'll be ready for success."

Actually, that's sound advice for any endeavor. You can benefit from being a student of someone else's experience, picking up not only technical skills and knowledge in your field, but an understanding of what it takes to be a leader.

Coach Smith understood what it meant to be under authority. As athletic director, John Swofford was Coach Smith's boss. I asked him if Coach Smith ever caused him problems. He quickly retorted, "Absolutely not!

"He respected my position," he continued. "Very successful coaches can make athletic directors' lives miserable, wielding such power and influence over alumni and others that our lives can be in constant chaos. This was never the case with Dean. He respected proper lines of authority.

"Whenever we disagreed, or he disagreed with the chancellor, it was always behind closed doors. We did have our disagreements, although not many of consequence. But you can imagine, at this level, there were times when I had to make decisions with which he didn't agree. How did he handle it? He was always respectful. Sometimes he would be forceful in his opinions, as I would hope he would be. However, when he left my office, he would either actively support the decision publicly or never state his opposition to it. He would never give negative publicity or the indication there was disunity. He was a person who understood what it meant to submit to authority."

Perhaps Coach Smith learned this principle from being an assistant under Bob Spear at the Air Force Academy and Frank McGuire at North Carolina. For example, no one can remember Coach Smith ever asserting himself against McGuire; he was completely loyal to him. In fact, during the years when McGuire's South Carolina teams were North Carolina's most fierce rivals, Coach Smith would always ask North Carolina fans to heartily and respectfully welcome McGuire back to Chapel Hill.

Or perhaps he took a page from Nordstrom's, which demands that every new worker starts at the bottom. If you're not willing to do whatever it takes to make a customer happy at the lowest level, from delivering a suit to a hotel room to getting on your knees to fit a shoe, you'll never be a leader in the organization.

However he learned it, Dean Smith understood that the best leader is the one who has learned to be under authority. I learned this truth through the most difficult time of my leadership. When I took this church through a new vision, it was very painful. People were highly critical. Some actually left the church. I shared in an earlier chapter that the healing of this very painful experience began when I went before the entire congregation, asked for forgiveness, and then began to build leadership consensus behind the scenes.

What I did not share, however, is what happened to lead up to that decision to go before the congregation. I was in a logjam with my lay leadership. I felt we should go in one direction. They simply weren't sure. I went away for a couple of weeks of vacation, confused about what I should do. My view of leadership at that point was that I was the leader, I received the vision, and they should follow. But it wasn't working. In fact, it was only alienating my lay leadership from me.

I then read a little book that said effective leaders in the twenty-first century will be people who have learned to submit to others and trust that the group can reach the right decision together. At first, I balked at the suggestion. How could I trust lay people to understand the right direction for the church? I was the one spending most all my time there.

They were only part-time. But the more I considered it, the more I knew the author was correct. I therefore decided to be a person under authority, to trust the process and believe that they, too, had the best interests of the church at heart.

I returned from my vacation. We scheduled our first meeting together. Tension filled the air. The lay leadership anxiously wanted to know what I would say. Finally, I told them about my time away and the book I had read. I told them I wanted to trust the process. I said, "I want to hear where you think the church should go. I am submitting to your wisdom." There was a stunned silence. That was not what they were expecting from me. They thought there would be more battles to fight. But it takes two to fight, and I had eliminated myself from the struggle.

What happened next was absolutely amazing. After several moments of stunned silence, one of the most influential leaders finally said, "Well, David, where again do you think we ought to go?" They gave me back my leadership. When I submitted to their authority, I was given authority in return. And we began together to hammer out the vision that, interestingly, was almost exactly the one I felt was right for the church. They were the ones who counseled me to appear before the congregation, apologize for my mistakes, and begin to work for consensus.

Leaders, when is the last time you willingly submitted to those over you? Did you publicly support the decision or pout? Did you seek unity above all else?

The Leader as Servant

Peter Drucker once said, "No leader is worth his salt who won't set up chairs." He meant that leaders who won't serve can't lead. Ken Blanchard, chairman of Blanchard Leadership and Training, and a popular author on leadership, had a similar view of customer service. "Customers are treated as if they really are the most important part of the business. Every employee and manager seeks to serve the customer or support those who do."

People are Coach Smith's most important product. He was and is extremely loyal to his players. He seeks to serve them. What many people don't know about Coach Smith, however, is how he has tried to care for many people he didn't even know. For example, my father was talking to the man painting my parents' house. Dad mentioned the book I was writing. The man then proceeded to tell about his father, a huge Carolina fan, who died of cancer. Coach Smith had learned of his condition, and one day while in Charlotte, he dropped by this man's hospital room unannounced. He brought a couple of players with him. For several minutes he cared for this fan, expressing genuine concern about his condition. The painter told my father, "He'll never know what that meant to my dad."

Coach Smith sees leadership as being a servant and putting others' needs first.

Equality for All

John Lotz thinks that a deep belief in equality motivated practically everything Dean Smith did, whether it was a religious, political, or athletic conviction. For example, the reason he treated the twelfth man on the team the same as the superstar is his belief that all people are created equal.

Coach Smith has been a champion for the cause of racial equality. Bill Chamberlain, one of the first African-American players recruited at Carolina, told me that even today when he becomes angry with racial inequality in America, he writes Coach Smith, sometimes just to get it off his chest. Every time he has written, Coach Smith replies, sensitively listening, encouraging Chamberlain to look at it from another perspective, or empathizing with his anguish.

In 1959 Coach Smith and his pastor took an African-American seminary student and sat down in a Chapel Hill whites-only restaurant. It was the first step toward serious integration in Chapel Hill. When asked about it, Coach Smith simply said, "It was the right thing to do."

Coach Smith recruited Charlie Scott, the first Carolina black athlete, in 1966. A year later Smith followed by recruiting Chamberlain, his second black player. Not until 1970 did Coach Adolph Rupp allow a black player on his team.

It was Coach Smith who asked John Thompson, a dear friend with a darker skin hue, to be his assistant coach for the gold-medal-winning USA Olympic team in 1976.

And it is Coach Smith who continually asks if the SAT is racially biased.

This commitment to equality, however, transcended his passion for racial justice. Everyone on the team, from the manager to the superstar, was treated fairly on and off the court, before and after graduation.

Donn Johnston, 1968–1972 letterman, is a Philadelphia lawyer who specializes in executive benefits and financial planning. He wrote to me, "I continue to use all of Coach Smith's principles on a daily basis. For example, treating everyone equally. It is very easy to focus attention on the individuals who bring business to the organization: the superstars. It is important for all to know there would be no superstars without those who work behind the scenes generating proposals, getting products out the door on a timely basis, and keeping the client happy when service issues arise. It is important to make these individuals part of the team and to demonstrate that their contributions are appreciated."

Leaders, do you see everyone in your organization as being created equally? How do you express your commitment to this principle beyond what the government demands? Do you show favoritism, partisanship? Has it destroyed your work environment yet?

Compassion for All

In the late 1980s Dean Smith spoke at a banquet I helped organize to raise money for an inner-city scholarship program. He hates to do that kind of thing. But he did. Was it because I was a former player and asked him to do it? Perhaps, yet he has turned me down on other offerings. I think he did it for one reason: it was a ministry to the poor.

Few will ever know his deep conviction to help the poorest of the poor. Heaven only knows how much time and money he has given to people and causes around the world to help clothe and feed the hungry and homeless. James Worthy said, "I remember receiving a unique Christmas present from him once. He sponsored a child in another country in my name. That really touched me."

Each Christmas my staff tries to discover a need among the poor of the world. We share this with our kids. We tell them that we may not have as many gifts under the tree because we want to help others in dire need. It has been a wonderful experience, keeping us in tune with the needs of others and helping us not be ungrateful and self-absorbed. We also ask each staff member to remember the poor throughout the year with special gifts and involvement. Several regularly go downtown to the soup kitchen to remind us of this responsibility.

If leaders only live in their nice homes without any reflection on the needs of the world, they most certainly will become hardened to hurts. Inevitably, that must be reflected in the workplace.

Coach Smith's generosity to the less fortunate extends far beyond an occasional project. It's more of a way of life for him; he is simply not money driven.

Carolina basketball teams travel first class on commercial flights or on planes chartered from NBA teams. They dine in fine restaurants and stay in the best hotels. But the team can afford to travel first class. The basketball program took in 7.2 million dollars last year and cost just 2.8 million to run.

Yet all this began to gnaw at Coach Smith. "I got to worrying that we were telling the players the wrong things by always staying in the best hotels or eating the biggest steak," he said. "I asked the players, 'Are we giving you the wrong message about materialism?'"

Smith was embarrassed by how much money he made — $162,750 in salary in 1997 before his retirement. When North Carolina signed a $4.7-million, four-year deal with Nike in 1993, Coach Smith made sure it covered 24 of the school's teams, although the athletic director said "this easily could have been a contract just for Coach Smith."

He received $500,000 from Nike as an up-front gift. Did he take it all and vault himself into the upper echelon of coaches' compensation? No! He gave away half of his annual $300,000 Nike salary, distributing it among his assistants and office staff. He also earmarked $45,000 of his annual salary for a special fund to be used by players who had yet to finish their degrees. He is even concerned for the three percent of his players who haven't graduated!

When John Kilgo hosted the Dean Smith Show on television, many businesses would approach him to ask him to convince Coach Smith to endorse their products. They would say, "He doesn't have to make a statement. We just want his picture alongside our product, and we will pay him a huge amount of money." Kilgo took these different offers to Coach Smith. Repeatedly he turned them down.

"But every other coach is doing it!" John said.

Coach Smith replied, "The professors on this campus would not be comfortable with the school's basketball coach making that much money doing something like that. I consider myself a teacher and it wouldn't be fair to receive that kind of money. It would send the wrong message."

Kilgo went on to say that Coach Smith made about one-tenth of what he could have made at North Carolina. All these opportunities were legitimate. "I kept pointing out to him that if the professors, even the chancellor, had an opportunity to do this, they would. But he wouldn't do it. He not only didn't want to make this kind of money, but he thought it was gross that anybody else did!"

When I asked Dave Hanners about Coach Smith's disdain for money and his silent generosity to those in need, he said, "Money is of no importance to him. He only drives a BMW because someone gave it to him. He doesn't care. I wish people knew how many times and for how many people, especially his former players, he has written personal checks to bail them out of trouble. I believe with all my heart that the only reason he desired to make any money at all was so he could give it away and help somebody else."

Terry Truax was a graduate assistant in the UNC program in 1971. He later was an assistant with John Lotz at the University of Florida, and subsequently became head coach at Towson State University, guiding them to the NCAA tournament on a couple of occasions.

Ultimately, Truax was let go from Towson. Between jobs, money was tight. One day, completely unannounced, came a check in the mail for $5000. It was from Coach Smith. A note was attached to the check saying that Smith had been unable to pay Truax much back in 1971. Now that he had some means, Coach Smith wanted to give the money to Truax in repayment for all his hard work at UNC years earlier.

As the cover story of *Newsweek* in February 1996 suggests, there's a struggle between lay-offs and CEO's salaries. Among the 12 corporations featured, 363,800 jobs were eliminated while the 12 CEOs together pocketed $19,736,011, not including stock options and benefits. What's wrong with this picture? Does this foster support or resentment? Doesn't resentment then pass over the remaining workers like the sword of Damocles? Isn't profit imperceptibly hurt even more in the long run?

Leaders, do you consider profit the means to the end or the end itself? Shouldn't money be the means to help people, who are indeed life's most precious commodity and important product? How does your salary compare with those who work with you? Is it highly unequal? Does this disparity create disunity?

A concern for the poor is not Coach Smith's only social concern. He has asked the NCAA to explore the integrity of having beer companies fund games and tournaments. With teenage alcoholism rampant and drunk drivers killing people by the thousands, in his opinion it's a bad image for college athletics to be associated with alcohol-related sponsors.

His wife Linnea, a psychiatrist, has asked Carolina preseason All-Americans to refuse to be a part of *Playboy*'s preseason picture of its All-American team. Coach Smith agrees. He thinks the magazine degrades women, and this is one way he can protest.

Coach Smith would be the last person to try and impose his beliefs on another person. He would say these social causes are very important concerns for him. However, I think he would challenge us all to see ourselves as a part of a larger community, to look at ways we can be a part of the larger good, individually and corporately.

Conviction Above Convenience

Perhaps the character trait of Coach Smith's that I admire most is his willingness to express his convictions no matter what the consequences may be. One of his firm convictions is that freshmen athletes should be barred from varsity sports so they can concentrate first on their academics. He believes athletes go to college to be students.

Smith opposed the rule change in 1972 that allowed freshmen to play varsity sports. When this change occurred, the competition for high school athletes intensified. Recruiting now begins in junior high school. This change also communicated to athletes the lie that college is a training ground for professional sports. Yet fewer than one percent of high school players get college scholarships, and fewer than one in a thousand go on to become professionals. In fact, most never even complete their degrees and consequently have nothing on which to fall back.

Coach Smith made the audacious proposal to permit freshmen to receive scholarships even if they sat out the first year altogether, allowing them to adjust to campus life and the rigors of academia. Then he proposed that these freshmen continue to receive full financial scholarship aid as they advance toward their degree.

Naturally, the dissenters say that the cost of this would be much too great. Yet this argument seems spurious when you think about the millions being generated by college athletics. For example, the major bowls are paying an average of eight million dollars to the teams and conferences playing in bowl games. Most schools are against the proposed rule because if they can recruit one great player, he can turn the entire program around.

Coach Smith furiously argues that part of the money made by these universities could be used to support freshmen athletes adjusting to academia. As he put it, "We would be saying, 'You're here as a student first. Once you've shown us your ability as a student, we'd be happy to have you as an athlete too.'" What's so interesting is Coach Smith and UNC would have been one of the nation's teams to benefit least from freshmen ineligibility. Since they were always getting commitments from the best high school players who would help the program immediately, to ask for freshmen ineligibility would certainly hurt UNC more than most other programs. But that wasn't the point. Coach Smith had strong convictions and they always held over convenience.

After Coach Smith retired, Bernie Linicome of the *Chicago Tribune* wrote: "He has been my coach...and everyone else's too, if they bothered to have one. It is not so much what he was — an innovator, if you count the Four-Corners offense, a tactic that once allowed North Carolina to beat Duke 21–20 — but it is what he wasn't. He was not a bully, he was not a cheat, and he was not a liar, the three items that lead the resume of most college coaches."

Dean Smith did it the right way, not with rage but with resolve, not with payoffs but with patience, not with intimidation but with inspiration.

Money, success, victory, and fame simply don't drive him. His conviction of character does.

Recruiting Character

Because of his own commitment to character, Coach Smith tried to recruit young men who also had character. He wanted good athletes, but he also wanted to recruit good people.

"We did look at a young man's character," he told me. "Indeed, if I had to do it over again, I think that would be even a bigger factor. I would not be so much concerned with his beliefs, but I would watch closely for his willingness to work hard, his tenacity to stay with a difficult situation.

"I probably would be willing to recruit more people like Hubert Davis. I told his dad he could maybe play for George Washington. Then he came here and was a first-round draft pick in the NBA. Sometimes we saw a player's court demeanor and walked away from him. There were probably some others in whom I saw potential problems but took them anyway because of their ability. Life is too short. I would probably make character an even higher priority in recruiting if I were doing it today."

How did he discover if a player had character? James Worthy revealed one of his secrets. "I was a blue chipper," Worthy said. "A lot of colleges wanted me. When Coach Smith came to visit me, I was wondering about playing time, if I was going to be a star, and if I'd get a pair of sneakers. The only thing he said to me is that I'd have to go to class unless I had a written permission slip from my parents. I also had to go to church each Sunday. 'That is what we do at Carolina,' he said.

"Later I realized he was recruiting character. He was looking for good players and good people. He knew these kinds of kids best played his philosophy."

Not only did he spend a lot of time with the parents on recruiting visits, but he would also watch a player's interaction with his parents. Did he show respect, for example? I imagine that while he spent so much time talking with James Worthy's parents, he was watching James's reaction. Was he irritated that Coach Smith wasn't speaking to him?

He also spent much time with a player's high school coaches. He valued their input on character. During games he closely watched how a recruit played — was he selfish or unselfish? — and how he spoke to officials, coaches, and teammates.

Perhaps the best example I could give of Coach Smith's ability to recruit character would be Bill Guthridge, his long-time assistant and eventual successor. Coach Smith gave the same detailed attention to recruiting assistants as he did players, and when he recruited Coach Guthridge, he made an outstanding choice.

The Charlotte Observer did a feature article on Coach Guthridge right after North Carolina won the ACC Tournament in March 1998. The article described Coach Guthridge's narrow escape from polio at age 11. Medical tests showed he had the virus but recovered quickly. One of his neighbors, a boy who lived four houses down, was not so fortunate:

> One morning when he was twelve, Bob Brandenburg didn't feel much like playing. The next morning he couldn't get out of bed.
>
> It could be devastatingly fast, polio.
>
> By the time school started in the fall, Brandenburg was in a wheelchair. The junior high was about one hundred yards away, up a slight incline. That first morning, as he looked out the window at the kids moving past, Brandenburg saw someone waiting in the driveway.
>
> Guthridge had come to push him to school.
>
> "I'd had polio a year earlier, so I could empathize," Guthridge says. "I think anybody would have been happy to help."
>
> "Bill was such a loyal person," Brandenburg says. "He pushed me to school the next six years."

Leonard Bernstein, the famous orchestral conductor, was once asked what was the most difficult instrument to play in the orchestra. Without blinking an eye he responded, "Second fiddle." Coach Guthridge loyally played second fiddle to Coach Smith for more than 30 years. But he had demonstrated his loyalty much earlier by pushing a friend's wheelchair for six years.

John Lotz, another long-time assistant in the 1960s and 1970s, also understood that Coach Smith recruited character in his assistants. "When he approached me about coming on staff, he knew the quality of my life. He knew my background and my character. He wanted someone to help recruit good student-athletes and be loyal to him. I enjoyed being that person, because I knew his character and knew that he would be loyal to me."

Dean Smith knew how to find players and coaches with sterling character. It's a valuable skill for a leader to learn, because recruiting character can make a tremendous difference in a positive work environment and production.

Thought for the Day

Before we can do, we must be.

Game Plan

- Humility

- Hard work

- Honesty and integrity

- Personal appearance and conduct

- Submitting to authority

- The leader as servant

- Equality for all

- Compassion for all

- Convictions above convenience

- Recruiting character

Team Practice

- How do you demonstrate honesty in your personal life?

- How do you demonstrate honesty at work?

- What happens when your beliefs are different from the beliefs of others in your organization?

MAKING FAILURE
YOUR FRIEND

"Look at your mistake,
learn from it, and move on."

The 1994 team was supposed to be one of Carolina's best ever. Four starters returned from the 1993 national championship team, and three gifted freshmen — Jeff McInnis, Jerry Stackhouse, and Rasheed Wallace — joined the team. But the players never jelled as a team. They lost in the second round of the NCAA tournament to an undersized and undermanned Boston College team.

In preparation for the next year, Coach Smith sent his players a copy of the front page of *Sports Illustrated* after the Boston College upset. It was titled, "A Talented Team Falls Flat." In the accompanying article, the writer said, "Smith, whose greatness is undeniable, may have done the worst coaching job of his career with the most talent he has had."

Coach Smith was unafraid for the team to read this criticism. Indeed, he wanted them to see this failure. He then challenged this team to be better, vowing he would be a better coach. The team was very successful that season.

I had originally decided not to write this chapter as a part of this book. Yet the more I though about all Coach Smith had taught me about life and leadership, it became increasingly apparent that I would be remiss if I failed to include it.

In fact, after I had almost completed the manuscript, I went to Chapel Hill to update him on the project. During our meeting, I mentioned that I wanted to write about making failure your friend. His response was immediate: "Please do it. That's a very important principle for me."

As we visited, Coach Smith recalled a particular day in practice when Matt Wenstrom did something wrong, and then started to pout.

Coach Smith went over to him and asked, "How do you handle mistakes in life?"

Wenstrom quickly recited the thought for the day from the practice plan. "When faced with failure, recognize it, admit it, learn from it, forget it!"

Coach said to all the players, "If you can learn any one thing in life, learn that! Learn from your mistakes and move on."

Someone once said, "You don't drown by falling in the water. You drown by staying there!"

Coach Smith's career was marked by many failures. But he continued to learn from them. He steadfastly refused to stay in the water and drown. Instead, he learned how to become a fantastic swimmer.

A question often posed at leadership and management training seminars is, "Are leaders born or made?" The answer must be, "both."

Leaders must be born with an innate intelligence and giftedness to lead. Coach Guthridge ventured his opinion on why Coach Smith was so successful. "What few people ever talk about is the fact that Coach Smith is an extremely intelligent person. So when you factor together his intelligence with hard work and preparation, and then learning from different failures in life, well, that equals a very successful coach and leader."

Leaders need an innate intelligence. However, we cannot miss Coach Guthridge's last comment that leaders must also learn from life's failures. Leaders are born...and made!

R.L. Johnson Jr., former CEO of Johnson and Johnson, profoundly stated, "Failure is our most important product." Indeed, its baby talc came about when Fred Kilmer, its director of research, responded to a physician's critical letter who complained about patient skin irritation from Johnson and Johnson's medical plasters. He simply sent the talc to soothe the skin and success was birthed!

Dean Smith learned many leadership skills in the fires of life's failure. We too often forget those early years, when he didn't win, when the critics said he would never win at college basketball's highest level.

We forget that students in Chapel Hill hung him in effigy in the early 1960s because he didn't win a big game. We forget that alumni wanted him dismissed during those early seasons.

We forget that for two decades critics said he couldn't win the big one, the national championship. When he finally did win it in 1982, they said, amazingly, that he probably couldn't do it again.

We forget that in the 1990s, before his second national championship in 1993, critics said the game had passed Dean Smith by and suggested he retire, allowing UNC to get a younger coach who could relate better to contemporary college players.

We forget that one rival ACC coach named his dog "Dean" because, the man said, "he cries and whines so much!"

We should remember all these things, because these failures and criticisms forged his character, strengthened his resolve, and forced him to grow as a leader. I think he knew that the fear of failure is the greatest enemy of success. Therefore, he learned to embrace failure. He learned to make failure his friend.

Tom Peters, the management consultant and best-selling author, urges us all to celebrate our failures, learn from them and, indeed, build on them. For him, failures are an essential part of progress. He said, "The essence of innovation is the pursuit of failure...to be able to make mistakes and not get shot."

He then quoted Soichiro Honda, the founder of the Japanese automobile of the same name, who said, "Many people dream of success. To me, success can only be achieved through repeated failure and introspection. In fact, success represents the one percent of your work which results only from ninety-nine percent that is called failure."

Or, as that inimitable philosopher, Dolly Parton, once said, "The way I see it, if you want the rainbow, you gotta put up with the rain."

Failure Does Not Have to Be a Foe

When we look at Coach Smith, the winningest coach in college basketball history, we tend to forget the losses. It's the same way with leaders in all walks of life.

The average American millionaire, for example, has been bankrupt 3.75 times. Henry Ford went broke on five different occasions before he finally succeeded.

Albert Einstein did not speak one word until he was four years old. He couldn't read until he was seven. One teacher described him as "mentally slow, unsociable, and adrift forever in his foolish dreams." Another called him "uneducable." The Zurich Polytechnic School refused him admittance.

The father of the famous sculptor, Rodin, once said to him, "I have an idiot for a son." His teachers described him as the worst pupil in the school. He failed three different times to gain entrance to the school of art.

Some of the world's most famous products were the results of mistakes: cheese, aspirin, paper towels, and penicillin, just to mention a few.

The man who dreamed up the photocopier thought he had discovered something wonderful to aid industry. He shopped his invention to IBM, Kodak, and RCA. They all scoffed at the idea and rejected it. Ready to give in to failure, he finally took the idea to Xerox. The rest is history. I can tell you that everyone on my office team appreciates the fact that he made failure his friend and didn't give up!

Dewitt and Lila Wallace had done a bit of everything from farming to DeWitt fighting and being wounded in World War I. He became a copywriter, but was fired. They finally came up with the idea of digesting much reading material into one magazine. They took the idea to several New York publishers. It was rejected by all.

So in 1921 they borrowed money and started the magazine in a small room beneath a speak-easy in Greenwich Village. More than three-quarters of a century later, *Reader's Digest* sells almost 28 million copies per month. For those of us with limited time, we're glad that the Wallaces made failure their friend.

Failure can be a leader's most formidable foe, but it doesn't have to be.

Walt Disney was abruptly dismissed by a newspaper editor for whom he worked. What was the reason for the dismissal? The editor said Disney lacked new, creative ideas. Disney was also personally bankrupt several times before he finally came up with the new, creative idea of Disneyland.

In fact, few know that Disney had an animation business in Kansas City, Missouri, that went under. That's what caused his move to California. So in 1923, at the ripe age of 22, he moved in with his uncle Robert in Hollywood. Rent was $5 for room and board. However, soon Disney ran out of money. His uncle's patience waned and he was ready to send Disney to the streets. At last, a vaudeville-house operator finally agreed to sponsor a cartoon series.

Disney then constructed a simple wooden box in his uncle's garage. The cartoons were quite simple, just stick figures with the jokes printed in comic-strip balloons. Yet that was the start of Walt Disney's cartoon genius, now reaping profits annually of $22.5 billion.

Boeing went through difficult struggles in the 1930s, 1940s, and again in the 1970s after it had to lay-off 60,000 employees. Hewlett Packard had severe cutbacks in 1945. In 1990, its stock value dropped below book value. Ford suffered one of America's largest annual losses in the early 1980s ($3.3 billion in three years) before it began a new core value of people first. IBM was nearly bankrupt in 1914 and 1921, and experienced difficulties again in the 1990s. Many great people and companies suffer failure; they just know how to make it a friend.

Madeleine L'Engle wrote a children's book titled *A Wrinkle in Time.* My own children have read it over and over again. It's one of their favorites. But the book was rejected by more than 50 publishers before seeing print.

Vince Lombardi once had an "expert" say this about him: "He possesses minimal football knowledge. He also lacks motivation." This expert predicted failure for Lombardi as a football coach.

Winston Churchill failed the sixth grade. He twice failed to achieve an elected office during the early 1920s and had little political influence all through the 1930s. But he learned from his failures and kept developing his talents. In 1940 he became prime minister of England at the age of 62. Today he is acclaimed as a great leader and hero of World War II. The free world is certainly glad he made failure his friend.

A young man named Rocko wanted to become a big league baseball player more than anything else in the world. For years he tried to develop his skills. Finally he took a long train ride to Fayetteville, North Carolina, for a try-out with a major league team. He hit one double, but other than that his performance was uneventful.

On the long train ride home he felt great disappointment and was ready to give up. He asked a friend riding the train with him about boxing; Rocko thought he could be successful in that sport. His friend, Ray Gormley, said Rocko had no future in boxing and discouraged him from trying.

Yet he did give boxing a try, and he became a world champion. Millions of fans knew him as Rocky Marciano.

The Greatest American Failure

"There lies the most perfect ruler of men the world has ever seen...and now he belongs to the ages."

Which great world leader did this statement address? Alexander the Great? Winston Churchill? Julius Caesar? George Patton? John F. Kennedy? No, none of these is right.

Perhaps some background information would help.

When he was seven years old, his family was evicted from their home because of a legal technicality. As a result, he was forced to go to work in order to help support them.

At age nine, while groping to find his identity as a child and suffering from extreme shyness, his mother died.

At 22, he lost his job as a store clerk. He was therefore unable to secure the proper education to fulfill his desire to attend law school.

At 23, he became a partner in a small business enterprise but went into huge debt when his partner died and left him the debt to repay.

At 28, he asked a young lady whom he had been dating for four years to marry him. She declined. This was the second romantic disappointment for the man. An earlier youthful relationship had tragically ended when his love died.

At 37, after three unsuccessful attempts, he was elected to Congress. Two years later he tried for re-election, but was defeated. It was during this time he had what contemporary psychologists call a nervous breakdown.

At 41, during the time when his marriage was aching, his four-year-old son died.

At 42, he applied to be a land officer. He was rejected.

At 45, he ran for the Senate and lost.

At 47, he was defeated for nomination as the vice president of the United States.

At 49, he ran for the Senate again...and was defeated again.

During these long years of disappointment, critics circulated false rumors about him. Consequently, he suffered from long, deep periods of depression.

Yet, at 51, he was elected president of the United States, only to have his second term in office cut short by an assassin's bullet.

While he was dying, one of his chief antagonists, Edwin Stanton, spoke the statement previously quoted: "There lies the most perfect ruler of men the world has ever seen...and now he belongs to the ages."

Abraham Lincoln, one of America's most inspirational and gifted leaders, could in many ways be considered the greatest American failure. Yet he knew the truth that pain can lead us to possibilities and suffering can lead to success. He, too, allowed failure to be his friend, and the United States is a better nation because of it.

Every outstanding leader knows this truth: we learn much more from our failures than from our successes. It is in the pain of failure that we gain new insights about our weaknesses and how to succeed. Adversity becomes life's university.

Learning from Mistakes

In my own most difficult leadership crisis, Coach Smith's words about making friends with failure proved invaluable. Let me give you some background. I have been the leader of Forest Hill Church for 19 years.

About six years ago, after turning down an opportunity to lead another congregation, I felt the time was right to move the church in another direction. We had grown significantly in previous years, but most of the growth had come from people dissatisfied with other churches. Simply receiving another organization's dissatisfied customers did not connote health. I felt that for a church to be truly outreach-oriented, it needed to make more efforts to reach the unchurched. Besides, the disgruntled people often brought their own baggage and hurts from their previous churches. Eventually, they became angry with us, too.

With this in mind, I wrote a 70-page position paper that I felt would direct us into the twenty-first century. Forty of this church's significant leaders gathered together for a weekend and I enthusiastically cast the new vision. There was some discussion. However, in my zeal, I committed a huge leadership mistake. Beginning the second day, I said something like, "Well, I believe so much in this new vision that if you don't want to do it, I may have to go somewhere else."

I'm sure, in retrospect, that's not what I intended to say. Moreover, I'm certain I was undergoing some "aging and staging" in my life. I was in my early forties and was subconsciously applying leadership pressure to myself and the other leaders so the new vision could happen as quickly as possible.

However, I failed to realize that the leadership of the church felt bullied. They sincerely respected me, but they still felt bullied. They didn't tell me what they were feeling, however. Maybe they didn't want to hurt my feelings. Maybe they didn't know how to tell me. At the end of the weekend, they gave unanimous support for the new vision, although I didn't recognize their unanswered concerns.

As I aggressively moved ahead, casting the vision at every opportunity, more and more people felt alienated and hurt. It took months before I finally realized it. The people in the church simply were not moving in step with me.

During the next several months, several staff members left. One became pregnant. Another felt called to return to seminary for more graduate work. I had to let another one go. Another suffered a massive heart attack and died. Suddenly I had four staff positions open. I also had a new vision to which to recruit new staff. And that's exactly what I did.

We recruited all over the country and tried to find the best people possible. Over the course of the next year, all four staff positions were filled with gifted, aggressive, and excited people. With them, I moved ahead with the vision with great vigor.

However, I again failed to notice what was happening with my core leadership. They weren't on board. Maybe my head was in the sand. Maybe I wasn't listening. Maybe they didn't have the courage to state their minds. Or perhaps it was a mixture of all of the above. But a slow, rising tension began to engulf the church. Other members of the church were even accusing the leadership of not having the courage to confront me. No one trusted anyone else. Everything was grinding to a halt. My leadership was in trouble.

To be candid, I wanted to quit. Everything was failing. I was frustrated and tired. I didn't want to continue the fight. Yet amidst this struggle, I remembered the very important leadership secret Coach Smith taught me years earlier: make failure your friend. Look at your mistake, learn from it, and move on.

So when I finally realized the problem, I knew I had two options. I could continue to steamroll ahead and let the chips fall where they might. Or I could stop, go in front of the people, apologize for my mistakes, and seek their input.

I chose the latter. I recommitted myself to leadership. I devised a plan to find unity, a vision both staff and leadership could buy and support. I met with each lay leader for at least an hour, often more. I asked his opinion of what had happened. I quizzed him regarding how I had failed. I intently listened. I took copious notes. I told each one that anything about me or the staff was fair game. I really wanted to know what they were thinking.

Then, over the next several months, we got the lay and paid leadership together. With the help of a church member skilled in conflict management, we got people talking with one another. When they did, we were surprised to find that most of the problems were blown way out of proportion. The mistrust that had formed between us began to dissolve.

After several months of healthy dialogue, I then recommitted myself to them as a servant leader. I told them I wanted a common vision, one on which we all could mutually agree and enthusiastically support. I told them that if they wanted to tear to shreds the previous vision and start all over again, I would be willing to do that. Amazingly, they all looked at me and said, "You're the leader, lead us!" So we went over the vision again, took out some areas of weakness, and added other items that made it stronger. We ended with a stronger vision statement that could now be taken to the congregation with total unity.

Was it hard? Absolutely! Who enjoys eating crow? But I did regain their trust. When I retreated, consensus started building. Soon the church moved ahead with enthusiasm. Amazing growth began to occur, largely from those who had never gone to church.

That all happened several years ago. Today this church is one of the healthiest, fastest growing in the area. It is a purpose-driven organization. People genuinely care for one another as at no other time in my leadership here. Throughout the organization, people clearly know what we're about. The vision is easily articulated by almost everyone.

We learned through a very difficult episode that failure should not be feared. When properly approached, it can be one of life's best teaching tools.

Where There's a Way, There's a Will

Jim Valvano, the late coach of North Carolina State University, loved to tell this story about Coach Smith and the 1982 national championship game against Georgetown. During the timeout, with 30-plus seconds to go and UNC down by one point, Valvano was having fun with the Carolina fans surrounding him. He offered all of them different offensive strategies to score the winning basket and then stop Georgetown on its ensuing possession. One particular fan kept responding to each of Valvano's strategies, "Dean will find a way."

As most fans know, Michael Jordan scored the go-ahead basket with 16 seconds left. As Georgetown came down the court, Freddie Brown accidentally threw the ball to James Worthy; Carolina won the game.

Valvano stared incredulously at Brown's errant pass. Then the UNC fan tugged on his sleeve as the final buzzer sounded Carolina's victory. "See," he said, "I told you Dean would find a way!"

One of the ways Coach Smith always found a way was through the avenue of failure. It didn't scare him. It didn't intimidate him. It didn't cause him to worry. He simply embraced it and learned whatever he needed to know. The failure made him better.

Failure also made his players better, even Michael Jordan. Jordan once said: "I missed more than nine thousand shots in my career. I've lost almost three hundred games. Twenty-six times I've been trusted to take the game-winning shot, and missed. I've failed over and over and over again in my life. And that is why I succeed."

Jordan, like Coach Smith had found a way to make failure his friend. It's one of Coach Smith's secrets to success, and he wanted me to make sure I told you!

Thought for the Day

***When faced with failure, recognize it,
admit it, learn from it, forget it.***

Game Plan

• Do not fear failure — everyone makes mistakes

• Learn from your mistakes and move on

• Keep trying to find a way — there is one

Team Practice

• How do you deal with your mistakes?

• How do you help others learn from their mistakes?

• How does your organization deal with mistakes?

• What can your organization do to
encourage learning from failure?

KNOW WHO REALLY
IS IN CONTROL

"There have been many times in life when I've had to give up."

I used to have a favorite illustration about Winston Churchill, the esteemed prime minister of Great Britain. His skillful leadership kept England steady during the incessant battering of German air raids during World War II.

It seems that Churchill graduated in the bottom third of his school class. There was absolutely nothing special about his scholarship or leadership back then. But many years later, as prime minister, his alma mater invited him to give the commencement address. The story is that he walked to the podium and told the students, "Never give up. Never, ever, ever give up." And then he sat down. The stunned audience eventually broke into an uproarious ovation.

For decades, ministers and speakers have used this anecdote about Churchill to motivate people to keep on trying when faced with adversity. It used to be one of my favorites, too, until Coach Smith readjusted my thinking about it.

When I told him how much I liked the tale, he responded, "David, I hate that story."

"But why?" I just had to ask. I was puzzled that this master motivator would loathe an example of dogged determination that paid off in eventual victory.

"Because I have learned in my life that many times I have had to give up," he replied, "and give it to God."

As I reflected on this statement, I realized its truth. Sometimes you *do* have to give up; there's simply nothing else to do but to quit trying and realize that, ultimately, you are not in control.

Few people know just how difficult those early years were for Dean Smith as the head coach of North Carolina. He wasn't the winningest coach in college basketball back then; he lost a lot of games and became the frequent butt of jokes. Art Heyman, Duke's All-American during Smith's first two seasons, was amazed when he discovered how revered Smith had become. "Dean Smith?" he said. "Why, he was the biggest joke around."

Frank McGuire, under whom Coach Smith served as an assistant, used to joke about his name, taking a dig at a person he thought to be rather drab, a person of gray anonymity: "Dean? What's that? A guy's not named Dean. He becomes a dean!"

Larry Brown, probably the best player on those early teams, said, "I don't know many men who could have gone through those first few years." When Coach Smith was hung in effigy, the question on everyone's mind changed from "will he leave?" to "when will he leave, and who will be his replacement?"

During this painful time, Coach Smith's sister gave him a book by Catherine Marshall called *Beyond Ourselves*. He is particularly close to his sister, and she has a keen interest in spirituality and theology.

Helplessness Is an Asset

Coach Smith focused on one particular chapter, titled "The Power of Helplessness." He began to see how little in life he really could control.

Winston Churchill's very short, very dramatic never-give-up speech may be great fodder for motivational speakers, but life had taught Dean Smith that it simply wasn't true.

"Crisis brings us face to face with our inadequacy," Catherine Marshall wrote, "and our inadequacy in turn leads us to the inexhaustible sufficiency of God." That described exactly where Smith was: face to face with his inadequacy. "No sinner is hopeless; no situation is irretrievable. No cause is past redeeming," she said. "Helplessness is actually one of the greatest assets a human being can have...the crucible out of which victory could rise." Catherine Marshall's book had Coach Smith's full attention.

Before the next game against Duke in Durham, he gave a spirited talk to the team. That was unusual; it's just not his style to give fiery pep talks. But he motivated the players that day, and Carolina beat Duke, 65–62. Two years later he made his first Final Four.

No one but Coach Smith knows exactly what happened during those days after he was hung in effigy. In an article written about him in the magazine of the Fellowship of Christian Athletes, he refers to this tumultuous time in his life. He reflected how he went home after all this turmoil and told God that he had given his life to Him many years before. Now he was giving Him everything, basketball included.

He learned an important truth that many great leaders have learned in the darkest days of adversity: key men need to learn who really holds the keys.

Coach Smith recounted for me that time when he totally gave it all up and turned it over to God. It's a habit he still has. "I don't want to act like a saint, for I am not one," he told me. "But deep down, every day, I try to turn it all over to a higher power. I know I have to let go and let God guide me every day.

"I try to set some kind of example as a professing Christian, but I realize I fall far short. I choose the Christian faith because I know I am weak. I need help for strength and guidance. Of course, I believe all humans were created to feel inferior and weak until we creatures make contact with the Creator and learn that He is in control."

Life holds mysteries that only God understands. Coach Smith comprehends that. He realizes, as many of us do, that the most frequently spoken word in heaven is probably going to be "oh," when God reveals to us why He did what He did.

The philosophy that it is sometimes necessary to give up is summed up in one of Coach Smith's favorite prayers. It's called the Serenity Prayer, and he often gives a copy of it to people. Almost everyone is familiar with the first part of this prayer by Reinhold Niebuhr; here is the full version.

> God, grant me the serenity to accept
>   the things I cannot change,
> Courage to change the things I can,
> And wisdom to know the difference —
>
> Living one day at a time,
> Enjoying one moment at a time,
> Accepting hardship as the pathway to peace;
>
> Taking, as He did, this sinful world
> As it is, not as I would have it;
> Trusting that He will make all things right
> If I surrender to His will;
>
> That I may be reasonably happy in this life,
> and supremely happy with Him forever in the next.
> Amen.

Coach Smith always had a "thought for the day" typed at the head of each practice schedule. One of these little nuggets reads, "If you can't do something about a problem, it's a fact of life." Sounds like the Serenity Prayer, doesn't it? Accepting the things we cannot change is an important leadership principle.

Roots of Faith

Dean Smith was raised in a relatively strict family and church environment. His parents sowed the seeds of faith in his life at an early age.

They demanded that he attend Sunday services, sometimes spending most of the day at church. He went to youth camps at Ottawa University. During his high school and college years, his family belonged to the First Baptist Church of Topeka, Kansas.

Although his beliefs are no longer expressed in the strictness of his familial background, he still tenaciously holds to his faith in God. When Smith first moved to Chapel Hill, he joined a group of 25 people who began a new church in the area. The group committed themselves to racial justice and being a part of the lives of hurting people. That was the beginning, in the spring of 1959, of the Binkley Baptist Church. That congregation has had a tremendous effect on Coach Smith and his faith.

He attends church weekly, win or lose. He readily understands what Christianity is supposed to be about; therefore, he often gently criticizes the church at large for castigating wounded people, for not loving them unconditionally. He teases me that Alcoholics Anonymous probably understands how to create a loving community better than the church does.

"The purpose of the church," he said, "is to give people strength so they can move on with their lives. In my own congregation, we very much see it as a church headquarters. We gain strength from each other. Consequently, many of our members are in politics, and many are involved in bringing about social change. That's what the church should be doing — caring for one another so we can help a hurting world."

Although I am a pastor, I do not become defensive when he criticizes the church in this way. Dean Smith is right. It's all too easy for members of a church to get caught up in taking care of their own people to the neglect of the hurting souls all around them.

Sociologist Tony Campolo, who is often critical of the church, is a challenge and an inspiration to Dean Smith. Campolo urges followers of Jesus Christ to be concerned with the needs of the poor and oppressed worldwide while developing their own personal spirituality. Coach Smith has given me many of his tapes through the years, often saying to me, "You really need to hear this one!"

Yet his faith is also very private. Smith is not ostentatious about anything in his life. He follows the example recorded in Matthew 6 of Jesus, who instructed His followers to pray and give their money away, but to do it in secret. Smith desires no earthly recognition for what he believes is the right thing to do. He once said to me, "You know, David, you and I have the toughest jobs in the state of North Carolina. People vicariously live through how we perform. If we do well, they feel good about themselves. If we don't, they don't. Isn't that sad? Only God should be able to do that to our insides."

Expressions of Faith

After Carolina defeated Georgetown in 1982 for the national championship, Coach Smith gave some interesting insights into his faith in an interview with Wendy Ryan. He complained that athletic competition produces what our society calls winners and losers. "Those terms," he said, "certainly have different connotations which, in my opinion, isn't good. The 'loser' and those associated with losing sometimes feel bad, and the 'winners' have external affirmation for the wrong reasons. I don't think our Creator meant for one person or one group, the 'losers,' to feel bad in order for another group or individual to feel superior.

"The total emphasis on winning versus participation is the problem," he continued. "Why doesn't the Christian church invite the guy who dropped four touchdown passes to come and talk about his faith? The fact that so many want to interview me after the national championship instead of when our team has a bad year is an example of what I'm addressing. The Christian culture has adopted the secular culture's ideas of success."

In one of my meetings with Coach Smith, he related the story of a boxer who observed his opponent at prayer just before a match. The boxer anxiously asked his trainer if it meant anything. "Not if he can't fight," the trainer replied.

Coach Smith often struggles with athletes who credit God with all their success. "I have to admit that it bothers me when a Christian calls on the Lord as a celestial bellhop," he said. "Of course, a pro athlete may indeed perform better because his life-style as a Christian helps overcome anxieties experienced by other players. However, constant practice would help his performance the most.

"If Christianity promised a 'magic wand' to receive everything one wishes — such as perfect health or a perfect performance — one would choose Christianity for the wrong reasons. I believe God created each human being to have freedom of choice. If I choose to smoke three packs of cigarettes a day, then I should not blame God if I have lung cancer some day. If some drunken driver crosses the middle line and kills my son or daughter, I don't think that is God's will; it's the wrong choice of the other to drink and drive. So, if some athlete intercepts a crucial pass, that athlete has made a choice to practice and to use his talent. The quarterback throwing the pass may have prayed to have it completed."

One of Coach Smith's favorite authors, Robert McAfee Brown, said this about our freedom of choice: it is like we are all in a symphony, sometimes choosing wrong notes, and God, the Conductor, can still make beautiful music.

Although he is often open about his faith, Dean Smith would never force his faith on others. He honors their freedom of choice. He respects players from the Jewish faith. Within the last several years, he has had a couple of players with Muslim backgrounds. However, he did believe in what Danish philosopher and theologian Soren Kierkegaard called "the indirect witness." In his "thoughts for the day," published at the top of every practice plan, Coach Smith always tried to plant a seed that would last for a lifetime in the players' minds, something that could be all-inclusive for all faith perspectives.

James Worthy, one of Carolina's greatest players, remembers that Coach Smith used to be very open about conversation regarding his faith and seeing how his players' faith was developing. "But it wasn't something he forced on us," Worthy noted. "We said the Lord's Prayer before every game. That was a reminder to us, because in college you tend to forget those parts of your life. You aren't consistent with the way you were brought up. He was reminding us not to forget our roots.

"And before every meal he would mention faith. Because he wanted to remind us that something could always happen and we aren't in control."

Dean Smith sees coaching as a calling from God, in the classic sense of the word *vocation*. "My pastor, Dr. Robert Seymour," he said, "has helped me understand that any vocation is acceptable to God if it involves work that is necessary in God's world or work that makes a positive contribution to man's well-being and happiness. There is no double standard between sacred vocations and secular ones. Once I thought I had reneged on my promise to God to put Him first by pursuing a career in coaching. But now I know I can faithfully serve God as a coach."

Realities of Faith

After the 1982 national championship, Frank DeFord wrote an article about Coach Smith in *Sports Illustrated*. In the article DeFord explored why a few coaches felt Coach Smith was not real. One coach had even said, "The man and the image don't match."

DeFord spent a good bit of the piece examining Coach Smith's religious convictions, which go back to his Kansas upbringing. DeFord then pointed out how he thinks these spiritual roots were incompatible with Smith's divorce in the early '70s, the fact that he was a chain smoker, and that he enjoyed a glass of Scotch. He suggested this collision of faith with real life helped create an image, at least for some, of hypocrisy.

However, DeFord failed to realize several points of faith that frame Coach Smith's life. First, he never wanted to be seen as a saint. His faith became real to him through trials, but he still realized the constant struggle we all have in wanting to become what we are not.

Second, Coach Smith has never adhered to a rigid, fundamentalist position. He honors those who have chosen this path, but it is not one with which he is comfortable. The church he attends in Chapel Hill wears a "liberal" label. His Protestant Christianity never suggests that drinking is bad. Drunkenness is, and Coach Smith stands against that. But drinking alcohol itself is not against his religious convictions.

Third, he believes that faith is a journey. He does not believe he will ever be perfect in this life. He has never tried to be anything other than what he presents himself to be.

But DeFord also failed to realize that Coach Smith desires to learn from his mistakes and do better. Yes, his first marriage ended in divorce. It was an extraordinarily painful time. Yet he remains friends with his ex-wife, and they worked out a meaningful way of being involved with their children together. Moreover, his second marriage is solid, a loving union that produced two fine daughters. His mistress is basketball, and it may have cost him his first marriage; it hasn't his second.

As for smoking, he quit. Cold turkey. He knew it was destroying his health, so he abruptly stopped.

Does he still have foibles, besetting problems with which he struggles? Of course! We all do. But my purpose in these paragraphs is to point out how important his faith really is. It is my opinion that his faith informs practically all of the principles we have been addressing.

Foundation of Faith

Without understanding Coach Smith's faith perspective, you can't really understand why and how he operates. Consider these examples.

Why is he so loyal to his players? Why does he put them first? I think it's birthed in a spiritual conviction that we are to live this life first of all for others.

Why does he demand racial equality? It's because of his conviction that all people are created equal in God's sight; therefore we must do everything possible to make sure people are appropriately and fairly treated. Why did he begin recruiting black athletes in the mid-1960s? "When I became the coach at Carolina," he said, "my pastor advised me that I should recruit a black athlete. He thought most vocations are and should be *Christian* vocations, and as the coach my first responsibility in my Christian vocation was to have a black athlete in a predominately white southern university."

Why is cheating simply not an option for him? He has a firm conviction that taking what does not belong to you is wrong, and that the necessity of telling the truth is an immutable law of the universe, created by God to be obeyed by His creatures.

Why is the team more important than the individual? It's because of his conviction that community is very important. He believes that God created us to live together, and one way that can be learned and demonstrated is through team play.

Why care for the poor and oppressed? He follows the biblical example of feeding and clothing the hungry and reaching out to those who are suffering. His conviction is that we are all citizens of the world and responsible for one another.

Why not give into failure? It's because of the conviction that God is the God of the second chance.

Why is he such a positive encourager? It's because he has felt the positive encouragement from God to keep on going, even when the odds seem overwhelming.

Why the emphasis on self-effacement and humility? Because humility is one of the earmarks of the Christian faith and it therefore needs to be practiced as a way of life.

The list could go on and on. If you fail to understand Coach Smith's faith, you cannot understand the principles by which he lives. He believes God created the universe with certain underlying principles that define reality. God set them in motion and obeys them Himself. Coach Smith simply discovered them and used them in his own leadership.

Overriding Life Principle

One year Coach Smith and his wife spent each Thursday during the Lenten season with other church members studying a book entitled *Unconditional Love* by Father J.S. Powell. Powell asked a question in that book that had profound implications for his life: what is your overriding life principle?

"For some people," Smith said to me, "it is money, to some it is power, to others it isn't clearly defined as they look inward. The question I have studied is, 'What should be the motivation for turning a life over to God, or essentially to be a Christian?'... I have believed that the motivation for the Christian faith is gratitude. Gratitude for love and acceptance by God. Gratitude for forgiveness. Gratitude for giving us life.

"We can pray for and acknowledge gratefully the many resources of strength and courage and alertness which we receive as the gifts of God....Thus, as Christian laymen with athletic interests and talents, we see that anything we do, we do because God qualifies us to do it as we respond to the gifts he has given. Each of us then has a sacred calling."

A friend of mine in Charlotte is Greg Keith, a very successful developer who was a high school All-American and recruited by many schools across America, North Carolina included. Keith recently shared with me a conversation he had with Coach Smith during the recruiting process. Coach Smith said to him, "You know, Greg, you can't take God out to dinner, or to a sporting event, or any other place. But there is one thing you can always do for God and that's love His children. Whenever you do something good for His children, you are serving Him."

Keith remembers something else Coach Smith said: "God is sovereign over His universe. I am not in charge. He is. It rains on the just and the unjust. We're all returning to dust one day. Until then, we simply do the best we can for other people."

This is the kind of faith that allowed Dean Smith to withstand the critics for 36 years.

It's the foundation for caring for others before himself, placing the team before the individual, and building personal character. It's essential to understanding his greatness and effectiveness as a leader.

It's rooted in the wisdom of knowing when to give in and give it to God.

Thought for the Day

*Helplessness can actually be an asset,
the crucible out of which victory can rise.*

Game Plan

• Accept the fact that you can't control everything

• Have a sense of God

• Discover your vocation, your sacred calling

• Let your faith permeate your life

• Never force your faith on others

Team Practice

• What does having a sense of God mean to you?

• How do you demonstrate your spiritual beliefs in your personal life?

• How do your spiritual values impact your behavior at work?

• What role does spirituality play in your organization's success?

THE MARATHON
OF INFLUENCE

"It's daily living that really matters."

The Tar Heels had just suffered a heartbreaking loss in the first round of the NCAA tournament in 1979. On the bus ride back to Chapel Hill, a great silence fell over the passengers. The sense of failure for the highly ranked Tar Heels consumed the players' attention.

What did Coach Smith do? He went to the back and spoke to Ged Doughton, who had just played his last collegiate game.

"Come by the office first thing Monday morning, Ged, and let's start talking about your future."

That's typical of Dean Smith. Putting failure behind him, putting his players and their future first. Coaching for the long haul, not just a winning season.

Contrast his style of long-term leadership with someone like Al "Chain Saw" Dunlap. A month shy of his second anniversary as embattled Sunbeam's supposed savior, Dunlap was fired as chairman and CEO during a weekend meeting. The chairman who followed Dunlap said, "We lost confidence in his leadership."

Dunlap entered Sunbeam as a corporate superstar with a reputation for turning around a corporation with a sagging performance. How did he receive the nickname "Chain Saw"? He was known for coming into a corporation and slashing thousands of workers in a cost-cutting effort during his 15-year career. He prefers to be called "Rambo in pinstripes," but the expression "dunlaping" became a synonym for downsizing and layoffs.

At Scott Paper, where he cut a third of the workforce, the company's stock tripled during his 18-month tenure. Sunbeam's shares soared nearly 60 percent the day Dunlap's hiring was announced. At Sunbeam, Dunlap cut 6000 jobs, half the workforce. He shut down 18 of 26 factories.

When word of Dunlap's firing spread, none of Sunbeam's former workers felt sad. In fact, they couldn't hide their happiness. They were ecstatic that the "Chain Saw" had been sawed in two.

Some of the 500 workers laid off from an iron and toaster plant Dunlap closed in Louisiana were "doing cartwheels," said Gary Elliot, a former maintenance manager. He said, "You never want to gloat when someone is terminated, but he affected a lot of lives here. Ours was a profitable plant. He closed it purely to boost the stock. He got what he deserved."

Dunlap is not the only corporate superstar whose brilliance has faded. A physicist who had previously turned around ailing National Semiconductor, Gilbert Amelio lasted 17 months at Apple before being fired and tagged with the label "plodder and technocrat."

AT&T President John Walter, after much previous success, lasted only nine months, unable to build consensus and gain the support of the board.

Hollywood's super-agent, Michael Ovitz, was sacked by Disney after a short time. In the midst of Wall Street's bull market, you must have a corporate scapegoat when performance is lackluster. No CEO seems safe.

It's interesting that, shortly after joining Sunbeam, Dunlap told an interviewer that if a company couldn't be fixed in a year, it couldn't be fixed. He displayed the same arrogance in the title of his book about corporate restructuring: *Mean Business: How I Save Bad Companies and Make Good Companies Great.*

After Dunlap's dismissal, Sunbeam told its workers and shareholders that management was determined to turn things around. But one official, in trying to encourage people, asked for patience. He said, "We're in absolutely no hurry. We are long-term players."

A Contrast in Leadership

Long-term players versus corporate quick-fixers. That's the contrast in leadership between a "corporate genius" like Al Dunlap and long-term leader like Dean Smith. Dunlap was concerned about the profit line first, people second. Coach Smith was concerned about people first and wins second. Dunlap loved the spotlight and claimed it whenever possible. Coach Smith shied away from public adulation, always wanting the players and the team to receive it.

Dunlap looked for immediate results — fix it in one year, he said, or it can't be fixed. Coach Smith was a leader for the long haul, patiently, year after year, building his foundation on the core values of people first, the team above the individual, and personal character. Dunlap was nicknamed "Chain Saw" by his work associates and peers. Coach Smith was and is affectionately called "Coach."

What was the result of these two different styles of leadership? Dunlap was fired in disgrace; his underlings despised him. Coach Smith coached for 36 years and retired with universal acclaim; his underlings adored him.

Coach Smith understood that great leadership is a slow, steady process. And he stayed put in one place for long-haul leadership. Both Pat Riley, who coaches the Miami Heat, and Rick Pitino, head coach of the Boston Celtics, have recently written books on leadership. I've read both, and they are very good. However, the major difference between their styles of leadership and Coach Smith's is that Riley and Pitino have moved three or four times in the last 15 years. That's not necessarily wrong. But when you're in one place for 36 years and consistently practice positive leadership principles, you affect people for a lifetime.

W. Edwards Deming, whose principles transformed Japan from the post-World War II rubble to a contemporary economic superpower, says that we must first have a purpose or a mission and that it must have constancy.

Sam Walton, the founder of Wal-Mart, said, "I have concentrated all along on building the finest retailing company that we possibly could. Creating a huge personal fortune was never particularly a goal of mine."

That was Coach Smith. Successful leaders are building values and principles lived out over a long time. Walton says his success really began about 20 years into the business. He didn't look for windows of opportunity, but steadfast obedience over the long haul to his core values.

Since I have been the pastor of one church for 19 years, I've baptized babies, confirmed them, married them, and then baptized their own babies. It develops into a beautiful long-term relationship with a congregation, and an ability to impact people that only comes with being there for the long haul. People have the opportunity not only to hear your words but to see you live them.

Which has the greatest impact — long-haul leaders or quick-fixers? Obviously, leadership over the long-term impacts the most people and impacts them to a greater degree. As Collins and Porras point out in *Built to Last*, nearly all of the early leaders of visionary companies stayed at the helm for long periods of time (an average of 32.4 years). I believe Coach Smith led for the present team he was coaching, but also for the next generation, and the next!

A part of Coach Smith's genius is that his leadership was not a sprint, but a marathon. He was consistent, and he led with long-term goals in mind. And when he retired, it was on his own terms. He left on top. People did not want him to retire. They wanted him to coach for as long as he wanted.

Moreover, and this has been too often overlooked, he left the cupboard full for his dear friend and long-time associate, Bill Guthridge. Look closely at the way Coach Smith's retirement unfolded. All his leadership secrets shine forth again. Reciprocal loyalty. Putting people first. The team above the individual. Personal integrity and character.

Notice also he endorsed someone who shares his core values and will continue to live them throughout his contract. That's why I'm convinced Coach Guthridge's successor will also be someone in Coach Smith's domain. This insures the values that built the organization for his 36 years will continue to lead Carolina basketball for decades to come.

Many today marvel at Jack Welch's leadership at General Electric. But he was raised in GE. He knew the culture, vision and values. His successor will probably be a similar choice. In 1991, Welch said, "From now on, [choosing my successor] is the most important decision I'll make. It occupies a considerable amount of thought almost every day."

That's how Wal-Mart, 3M, Boeing, IBM, Johnson and Johnson, Mereck, and many other visionary companies have staying power and influence over the long haul. It's why Carolina basketball will continue to be successful well into the twenty-first century.

Leaving at the Right Time

Coach Smith's retirement did not catch his former boss, athletic director John Swofford, by surprise. For the last several years Smith had evaluated whether he had the energy and enthusiasm necessary for his players to do their best under his leadership. He had always said he would retire when October rolled around and he didn't feel he could give the team and the individual players what they needed to succeed. Finally, in October of 1997, he didn't sense that excitement and announced his retirement. Swofford said, "He did it just like he said he would. His entire life has been first class. He had to go out on top."

What does it mean for a leader to retire at the right time? Swofford said, "Whenever we talked about his retirement, he would say every time that it was really important to him that he leave the program in good shape."

Leaving the program in good shape meant several things. First of all, from Coach Smith's perspective, it meant leaving the program in better shape than when he began as a leader. Looking back to 1961, when he became the head coach, that certainly occurred. The program is in much better shape now. Every effective leader should be able to see that kind of marked improvement.

Second, it meant leaving the cupboard full for his successor. Coach Smith has a deep and abiding friendship with Bill Guthridge. He wanted Coach Guthridge to have the job after his retirement both to reward him for all the years of faithful support and to give him a chance to earn enough money in a short period of time to insure his financial security. However, and perhaps even more important to Coach Smith, was to allow his loyal associate to succeed at the same level or perhaps even a greater level of success than he had.

John Kilgo, editor of *Carolina Blue* athletics magazine, is absolutely convinced that Coach Smith would not have retired in October 1997 if Antawn Jamison had decided to go professional after his sophomore year. When Jamison returned for his junior year, Coach Smith knew the team would be very good. The year before they had gone to the Final Four and four of the five starters were returning. Yet without Antawn, the team certainly would not have been as good. Kilgo believes that Coach Smith would have persevered through another season until the team would have been excellent enough to pass on to Coach Guthridge.

After Coach Smith's retirement was announced, Henry Araton wrote in *The New York Times*: "Of course Dean Smith has never admitted this, never will, but the coach with a record of 879 wins turned what might have been a grand farewell tour with a championship cherry on top into an extraordinary show of appreciation for a man who stayed by his side for thirty years. Smith thanked Bill Guthridge for his assistance in a way so many others in this look-at-me industry absolutely could not. Telling a half-truth that he was too tired to continue, Smith gave Guthridge a team to run with....To many, Smith was the 1997 Sportsman-of-the Year after breaking Adolph Rupp's record of 877 victories before losing to Arizona in the national semifinals. One year later, without being part of a single game, Dean Smith looks like a bigger sportsman than ever."

This says much about Dean Smith's character, doesn't it? In a day when coaches jump to the next university in order to receive the largest amount of money and acclaim possible in the shortest amount of time, here is an example of longevity, perseverance, success, and a concern that his successor experience equal benefits. Even in his retirement, Coach Smith was putting others first.

That was one of his major core values. It drove him. Like Walt Disney, who left his core values in place, allowed Michael Eisner and the new Disney team to resurge with prosperous success in the 1990s.

Contrast Disney to Columbia Pictures and its head, Harry Cohn. After his death in 1958, Cohn did not have these core ideologies in place. He didn't care first for people, and his funeral represented a Dunlap-like relief that he was gone. Someone at the funeral supposedly said that 1300 people came not to mourn his death but to make sure he was dead! Columbia limped along and finally ceased to exist as an independent company, rescued in 1973, eventually sold to Coca-Cola.

On April 11, 1997, headlines in the Chapel Hill daily newspaper proclaimed a startling announcement: Molly Corbett Broad became the first woman ever appointed to head the University of North Carolina's 16-campus system in the school's 200-plus-year tradition.

When asked about her leadership style, she said she followed the example set many years before by her faculty advisor, who was later a university chancellor and eventually one of her closest friends. "He was a great mentor," she said, and in today's vernacular he would be called a 'servant leader.'" Broad continued to explain, "His style was very humble, but he had a very strong conviction that his assignment was to turn the university over to his successor better, stronger, and healthier than he had received it."

I would imagine that Molly Broad sincerely appreciated Dean Smith's retirement. I only wish she could have watched his leadership. I believe it would have profoundly impacted her, as her chancellor friend similarly did.

When it comes to knowing when is the right time to leave, here are some questions that naturally arise.

Is the organization I am presently heading better now than when I first became its leader? If not, why not?

If it is better, what's the next stage to which my leadership is being called? Is it in this organization? Is it to another work?

Am I nearing the time to retire? Am I still feeling the same passion for my work?

Am I giving my work associates and my team my best energy? If that energy is beginning to wane, when should I step down?

Who should my successor be? Am I choosing a time for retirement that gives him or her the best opportunity to succeed, perhaps even beyond my own success?

After Coach Smith's retirement, Bill Guthridge gave me these insights regarding why Coach Smith finally retired. "He just didn't have the energy to coach the 1997–98 team that he knew it needed. And I think a lot of those energies went to former players and in many respects that just wore him down. I personally don't know how he lasted as long as he did. Because of the number of people that he cared about and was trying to help out overwhelmed him.

"When I was his assistant, I deferred as much of that as I could so he could concentrate on the big things, but I couldn't shield him from everything. No one knows the demands on his time, the long hours of work and the people he genuinely cares for. I don't know of another person who could have managed all of this, but he did."

Perhaps one of Coach Smith's most meaningful letters he received upon announcement of his retirement came from Dickson Gribble, a former player from his first seasons as head coach at North Carolina and presently a colonel in the United States Army. He wrote:

> Coach Smith,
> I am saddened by your retirement, but understand. As my own mandatory retirement date (30 years active duty) soon approaches, I often reflect on what's next. You alone know when you are ready — you alone. I admire you for knowing when it was time and doing it the way you did.
> Having been a part of an organization and a culture for so long that passes leadership, I reflect on it often. And I am often asked to speak about it. Even in military work, I use you often as my example. Note I didn't say always, in that I have had my life also cross with Colin Powell's. I cite your commitment to excellence, to integrity, and to caring for others as specific traits worthy of emulation. I often note your commitment to equal opportunity has been a part of the Carolina program since during the days of Willie Cooper and Charlie Scott.

I also talk about the importance of teamwork in my successful organization — be it on the sports field or battlefield. People understanding their role — as a soldier, civilian, point guard, or bench player. At Carolina, you taught us that we all had a role and to fill that role to the best of our ability for the overall benefit of the team. Thanks for that.

On his deathbed, Walt Disney purportedly was giving counsel to another leader about how to make Florida's DisneyWorld more successful. I can imagine Coach Smith doing something like that, on his deathbed, giving the present head coach insights into how to make UNC's basketball program even more successful. That's because he sees leadership for the long haul, not just for one year or several seasons.

As news of Coach Smith's retirement spread around the university, hundreds of students gathered outside the Smith Center. At the press conference to officially announce the retirement, they all chanted, "Four more years! Four more years!"

It was a fitting tribute to a coach who knew, perhaps better than anyone else, that winning wasn't nearly as important as how you play the game.

Thought for the Day

Leadership is a marathon, not a sprint.

Game Plan

- Think of influencing people over a lifetime
- Plan for your successor
- Know when to leave
- Leave your successor with success
- Imagine what people will feel at your retirement...and funeral

Team Practice

- What actions do you take to change daily inconsistencies?
- What should be done to plan for a successor?
- When should that be?
- Would your successor succeed?
- How would your underlings feel at your retirement and/or funeral?

When talking to different people for this project, I concluded each interview with this question: "Pretend Coach Smith is right here in front of you. You now have the opportunity to tell him anything you desire. What would you say to him?"

Here are their answers.

> "Coach Smith, I've always told you I've appreciated you. I also want to say I love you for what you have done in my life. It's meant a lot to me and to generations of young people who will be influenced by the people you have touched."
>
> **—Bobby Jones**
> athletic director and head basketball coach
> Charlotte Christian High School
> Charlotte, North Carolina

> "Thank you for the impact you have had on my life, from the first day I walked into your office to this moment. I want to say 'Thank you' because everything that I do in terms of my professional career I look back and think what would you do, then I try to do it like you."
>
> **—Justin Kurault**
> former team manager

"You are like a father figure to me, someone I really care about. I can't adequately express how much I appreciate you. God has used you in my life. I give God the glory, but He used you to get my marriage back in order and for me to be the right father to my children. You have even helped me out of some difficult financial situations. The best way I can say 'thank you' is to keep my life disciplined and to leave situations better than when I first got there."

> **—Al Wood**
> former UNC All-American

"Dean, you're an inspiration to so many of us and I appreciate what you represent not only to intercollegiate athletics, but what you represent as a human being."

> **—John Swofford**
> commissioner
> Atlantic Coast Conference

"I have always been surprised about the absolute reverence your former players have when they speak about you. When I spend time with you, I want to spend more time with you. When I am around you, I feel your goodness, your honesty. Thank you for who you are."

> **—Jerry West**
> general manager
> Los Angeles Lakers

"You are an amazing person. I know you don't want to take the credit, but there are a few of us out here that you are responsible for making us who we are. I love you like a father and I love you like a brother. And I just want to say thank you. You are the man!"

> **—James Worthy**
> former UNC All-American

"I am hoping to be a head coach one day, and I hope I can be one-hundredth of the man you are. I hope I can instill in my players all the values and all those characteristics that you instilled in me. I hope I can teach them about loyalty, friendship, integrity, and how to win and lose graciously, about saying nice things about other people, about saying thank you. Thank you for all you have done for me."

—Pat Sullivan
former UNC player

"Thank you for a terrific ride that you've let me go on with a lot of your teams and a lot of your different players. But more than that, thank you for what you've taught me about life in general. And how to be fair with people. You've taught me how to say things to people they may not want to hear but need to hear. Thank you for your compliments of my broadcasting. Thanks so very much for all you've done for me and all the young people who have played for you and all you've done for the university. It certainly would not be what it is today without your input."

—Woody Durham
"Voice of the Tar Heels"

"On behalf of all the coaches, players, trainers, secretaries, doctors, and anybody that has ever had a chance to associate with you, thank you. I don't know how you found the time to do it. To be such a good person in this profession is very difficult to do. It just shows what a wonderful human being you are."

—Eddie Fogler
head coach
University of South Carolina

"Well, first, I want to thank you very much for giving me an opportunity just to be a part of the North Carolina family. I also want to thank you for contributing so much to so many people's lives. You probably can't imagine how many lives you have touched, how special you are. We miss you and want you to continue to enjoy yourself because you've given so many people joy for a number of years."

> **—Jimmy Black**
> UNC starting point guard
> 1982 National Championship team

"I am a better person simply for being a part of your life. You made us all feel special. Thank you for who you are."

> **—Dave Hanners**
> assistant coach
> University of North Carolina

"Coach, you have been one of the most important people in all my life. Thank you for all you have meant to me through the years."

> **—Richard Vinroot**
> former UNC player
> former mayor of Charlotte, North Carolina

"You are a fantastic person. I would never be the person I am today if it were not for you. Thank you for all you have meant to me."

> **—Pearce Landry**
> former UNC player

"You are my friend. Your life has profoundly affected mine. Thank you for always being there for me.

—**John Lotz**
former assistant coach
University of North Carolina

"I appreciate everything you have done for me. Thank you for the care and concern you have shown for my family. Thanks for the steps you have helped me take, from East Tennessee State to N.C. State to here."

—**Buzz Peterson**
head coach
Appalachian State University

"No one can ever repay you for all you've meant to me and so many other people. You're an unbelievable man."

—**John Kilgo**
Editor
Carolina Blue

"Coach, thank you for all the great experiences I had as a player and a student at the University of North Carolina. You've been great to me, and I hope you're enjoying time off with your family."

—**Matt Doherty**
UNC starting forward
1982 National Championship team
head coach, University of Notre Dame

"Coach Smith, you have given me a lot over the years. You have helped me with major decisions in my life, and I would just like to thank you for that."

—**Charles Waddell**
last three-sport letterman at UNC

"I think the very best thing you can say about another person is that the more you get to know him, the more you like him. Dean, that's how I feel about you. And that's what I say to anyone who asks me about you. We're good friends and I genuinely like you, especially the more I've become acquainted with you."

—**Bob Knight**
head coach
Indiana University

"Coach, you're like a father to me. There is probably not a day goes by that I don't look back on my time at Carolina or a word from you that continues to help me in my life or in my family or in my community. I've always joked with my wife that the best decision I ever made was going to Carolina and she says, 'No, the best decision you ever made was marrying me.' So we get in a fight all the time because of you!"

—**George Karl**
head coach
Milwaukee Bucks

"I just want to say 'thank you' and that there is no way Roy Williams will ever be able to put into words what you mean to me."

—**Roy Williams**
head coach
Kansas University

"Coach, it's hard to pinpoint one thing. But I really don't know where I'd be today without you in my life. You're a steady rock who is always there for us. You give and give and give all the time. You do it because it is the right thing to do. You're a great basketball coach, but an even better human being."

—**Phil Ford**
assistant coach
University of North Carolina

"Thank you, and that's about all I know to say to you. I don't think you would want me to say much more than that. But that's enough."

—Bill Guthridge
head coach
University of North Carolina

And, finally, I have thanks of my own to offer.

"Coach, I'm who I am today partly because of you. I'm grateful I attended North Carolina and had you as my coach. The leadership principles I use that have allowed me to grow personally and lead Forest Hill Church to a position of prosperity I learned mostly from you — directly and by observation. Thanks for caring for my mom and dad and my own family. My life has been deeply enriched by knowing you...and writing this book! Thanks again for letting me do it."

Wouldn't any leader be deeply touched by having this said by former work associates at his retirement? Why would we say this?

The answer is undoubtedly found in this final word from Dean Smith.

In my last interview with him, I invited Coach Smith to look in the camera and tell all of us any one thing he'd like to say. He paused, a wry smile crossing his face. He pointed to the camera and said, "I'd say, 'Thanks for the pass.'"

And I'd say that appropriately sums up everything in this book, wouldn't you?

INDEX